Let the River Flow

A Native American Tale

adapted by Michael Sandler
illustrated by Siri Weber Feeney

Harcourt
SCHOOL PUBLISHERS

Printed in Mexico

ISBN 10: 0-15-351657-7
ISBN 13: 978-0-15-351657-3

Ordering Options
ISBN 10: 0-15-351215-6 (Grade 5 Advanced Collection)
ISBN 13: 978-0-15-351215-5 (Grade 5 Advanced Collection)
ISBN 10: 0-15-358150-6 (package of 5)
ISBN 13: 978-0-15-358150-2 (package of 5)

3 4 5 6 7 8 9 10   126   12 11 10 09 08

CHARACTERS

Narrator

Chorus

The Llanero

Ogarto, the Llanero chief

Kello, the chief's granddaughter

Alo, another Llanero

The Naisha

Hork, the Naisha Chief

Helok, the chief's younger brother

NARRATOR: It is feast time again. Two Native American tribes—the Llanero and the Naisha—have come together to celebrate. They celebrate their successful harvest. They gather to praise the mighty river, the river that provides water for their farms.

3

CHORUS: We live in a dry land. Without water from the river, nothing would grow. Our land would be uninhabitable. No one could dwell here. The Llanero people thank the river. The Naisha people thank the river. We celebrate the friendship of the people.

NARRATOR: At the feast, special foods are served. Special songs are sung. Contests are held between the two tribes. The two peoples live on opposite sides of the river. The Llanero live on the north side. The Naisha live on the south side.

CHORUS: The wrestling match will take place soon. The champion of the Llanero will wrestle the champion of the Naisha.

OGARTO: Come, Kello. Come, Alo. Let us go find a good place to watch the match.

KELLO: I hope the Llanero win.

OGARTO: Sometimes we do, sometimes we don't. Alo lost a tough match one year.

ALO: Somehow Helok beat me. The memory still hurts. It doesn't matter, though. Helok is my friend. All the Naisha are our friends.

KELLO: Have they always been our friends?

OGARTO: Yes, granddaughter, except for one difficult year. That was the year when the river failed to flow.

KELLO: The mighty river?

OGARTO: One year, the river wasn't mighty.

KELLO: Please, grandfather, recount the tale. Tell us what happened that year.

NARRATOR: Hork, the Naisha chief, arrives with his brother, Helok.

HORK: Tell her, Ogarto, the story of the year that the river failed.

OGARTO: Ah, Hork, I see you and your brother are here to root for your champion.

HELOK: He is the best wrestler the Naisha have had since me!

HORK: As long as we are here, we will help you tell Kello the tale. After all, we were responsible for the troubles.

OGARTO: No, Hork, nature was responsible. It was many moons ago, Kello. I was younger, much younger.

HORK: You had just become chief of your people, Ogarto. I had just become chief of mine.

OGARTO: Spring had not yet come. It was winter, a time when the river is always just a trickle. As you know, Kello, the river grows wide and strong only in the spring.

ALO: We looked at the mountains to the east. Usually, they were covered in snow. That spring they were bare. It had been a dry winter. Very little snow had fallen. It was a terrible sign.

KELLO: Why, Alo?

OGARTO: The river begins in the mountains, Kello. Most of the river's water comes from melting snow. Without snow to feed it, we knew it would stay a small trickle.

KELLO: Without water, our farmers wouldn't be able to grow crops!

OGARTO: Indeed, Kello. I knew a hard spring was coming, so I had the men dig a lake. We would fill the lake slowly and store water for the planting season. It might give us enough to produce a small harvest, even if the river stayed small.

HORK: As you know, Kello, the Naisha people live on the other side of the river. We also live downstream. From our land, we cannot see the mountains. We didn't know that the mountains had no snow.

HELOK: All we knew was that the river stayed a trickle in spring. We didn't have enough water for our crops. The seeds that we planted never burst to life.

OGARTO: On our side, small plants poked up through the soil. We carefully fed them water from the lake. The year would still be hard. If this crop grew, however, we would survive.

HORK: However, the fields of the Naisha tribe were parched. Nothing grew at all.

CHORUS: Come to the ring. The wrestling match is beginning. Two brave wrestlers are going to do battle. They represent the best of each people.

NARRATOR: Ogarto pauses in his story. The group takes its place to watch the contest. It is a hard struggle. Both athletes practice good sportsmanship. In the end, the Llanero wrestler wins. The two wrestlers shake hands. People of the Llanero tribe shake hands with members of the Naisha tribe.

OGARTO: This is how it should be—two different tribes respecting each other.

HELOK: Sadly, it wasn't like that in the year of the trouble.

HORK: I was suspicious. I didn't trust the Llanero. Why had our river almost vanished?

HELOK: Hork sent me to spy on Llanero land. I saw their farms teeming with small plants. We didn't have water. Somehow the Llanero did. We decided that the Llanero were somehow stealing the river's water.

OGARTO: Then you came up with your plan.

HORK: Yes, that's right. We traveled up the river. Then we began to dig a channel along the south side of the stream. It was a huge endeavor, two weeks of monotonous digging.

HELOK: I would know. I was in charge of the task. My arms ached so badly. At the end of each day, my eyes were brimming with tears from the pain. Also, I recoiled in pain each time I elongated my body to reach for something.

KELLO: Wait. Let me make sure I understand what happened. You dug a whole new channel for the river?

HELOK: That's what we did. Now the water flowed straight to Naisha territory. It wasn't much, just a trickle, but it was ours.

OGARTO: Of course, the Llanero noticed right away. Suddenly, the river was dry. It had been just a trickle, but now there was no water at all.

HORK: Now it was your turn to act.

OGARTO: We had no choice. We knew the water in our lake wouldn't sustain us for long. We walked up the river and found the new channel. We saw how the Naisha were draining the stream.

KELLO: What did you do, grandfather?

OGARTO: Just what the Naisha had done when they thought we were stealing the water. We dug a new channel.

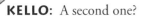

KELLO: A second one?

OGARTO: Yes, even further upstream. Now all the river's water came to us to replenish our water supply.

KELLO: What did the Naisha do then?

HELOK: We dug a third channel. Naturally, the Llanero dug a fourth. On and on it went, all through the summer. So much wasted work. So much wasted effort.

OGARTO: In the end, it almost ruined both the Llanero and the Naisha. You see, Kello, the river was just a trickle anyway. Each new channel wasted more water. It sank into the earth. It dried up in the sun. The new channels became clogged with debris.

HORK: In Naisha territory, people were nearly dying. Everyone was yearning for a drink of water. In Llanero land, the precious crops nearly withered away.

KELLO: Why didn't you just agree to share the water?

OGARTO: It seems simple to you, Granddaughter, but things are seldom so easy.

HORK: We were not thinking. We were stubborn. It took us so long to see the way. One day, Ogarto and I met up at the base of the mountains. We had each traveled to the birthplace of the river. There was nowhere further to dig new channels.

KELLO: What happened then?

OGARTO: We argued, bellowing loudly. I blamed the Naisha for starting the trouble.

HORK: I blamed the Llanero for starting it.

OGARTO: Then I realized that the Naisha didn't know the real cause. They didn't know about the lack of snow. I explained to Hork what had happened before things got too rowdy.

HORK: We were so ashamed and sorrowful. We had not conducted ourselves in our usual dignified manner.

HELOK: Suddenly, we knew what we both had to do.

ALO: The Llanero and the Naisha worked side by side. We closed off all of the channels. The river ran back the way it always had before.

HORK: It was still just a trickle but just enough for everyone to survive.

ALO: The Naisha people helped the Llanero tend the small gardens. They provided just enough food for all of us to get through that terrible, terrible year.

KELLO: And the Llanero and Naisha have been friends ever since that time?

OGARTO: Through bad times and good. Each year we celebrate our friendship at this feast. Each year we celebrate the river that gives us life. Now we only battle in wrestling matches. Disagreement between us would be unfathomable.

CHORUS: Come to the dining grounds. It is time for the feast to begin!

OGARTO: Shall we go?

KELLO: Yes, Grandfather. Your story made me very hungry!

Think Critically

1. Why is the river so important to the Llanero and the Naisha?

2. What did the Llanero know about the river that year that the Naisha didn't?

3. How did the two tribes solve their problem?

4. How would the text appear differently if it were written as a story rather than a Readers' Theater?

5. Does this book remind you of other stories you have read? Which ones?

 Science

Drought Use the Internet or another library resource to find out about the devastating effects of a drought. How does it affect the environment? Summarize your findings.

School-Home Connection Tell a friend or family member about this story. Together, think about ways the Llanero and the Naisha could have avoided the problems they had.

Word Count: 1,474